by R.J. Kluba

Mike Botsko was born in August 1923 in Gary, Indiana. He excelled at drafting and drawing in his scholastic years, and especially liked to draw military aircraft fighters and bombers of that era. He was 19 years old when he enlisted in the U.S. Army in 1942, and volunteered for duty in the Air Force soon after.

The 8th Air Force's 305th Bombardment Group was activated in March of 1942 at Salt Lake City AB and trained in Utah, Washington and California for overseas duty with B-17 heavy bombers. General Curtis LeMay initially organized and trained the group, and first led the 305th into combat over occupied Europe in November 1942.

In January 1943, the 305th participated in the 8th Air Force's first raid on Germany. During their missions over the next 3 years, the group attacked naval facilities, factories, harbors, marshaling yards and industrial targets in Germany, France, Belgium and the Netherlands until the end of the war in Europe in May 1945.

In December 1944 and January 1945, the 305th participated in the Battle of the Bulge by striking enemy positions in the Ardennes Forest on the German-Belgium border. The group also supported the Allied airborne assault across the Rhine River in Germany in March 1945.

305th Bomb Group Markings

305 BG

B-17 Ball Turret Target Training

Gunner cadets trained in ball turrets suspended from a platform and aimed their sights on a simulated enemy fighter. The target moved in a complete arc and was "fired" upon by other turrets on the platform.

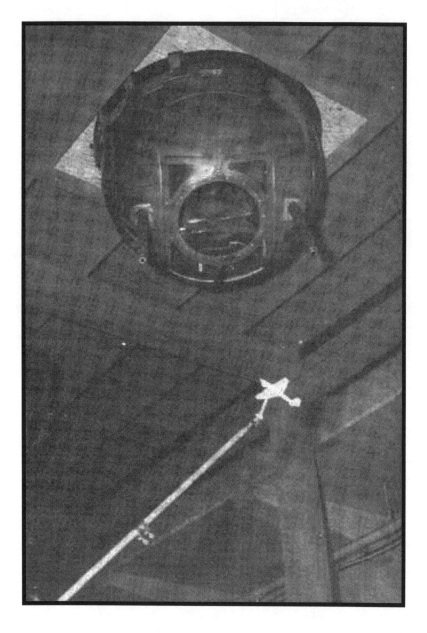

This book is dedicated to:

Members of the Crew

- **B. P. Brooks** .... **Pilot**
  Paris, Texas

- **R. A. Punzo** .... **Co-Pilot**
  Waltham, Massachusetts

- **M. P. Heilborn** .... **Bombardier**
  Greenville, Mississippi

- **F. G. Roberts**[*] .... **Navigator**
  Baltimore, Maryland

- **J. E. Pennington** .... **Engineer**
  Tulsa, Oklahoma

- **J. Ayala** .... **Radio Operator**
  Saginaw, Michigan

- **W.W. Schmitt** .... **Armorer**
  Dubuque, Iowa

- **M. Botsko** .... **Ball-Turret Gunner**
  Gary, Indiana

- **C.R. Bemis** .... **Tail Gunner**
  Athol, Massachusetts

- **W.D. Adamson**...................... **Extra-Gunner**
  Pasadena, California

---

* P.O.W. - bailed out over Berlin on December 5, 1944 and held captive at Stalag-Luft I in Nazi Germany until the camp was liberated by Russian troops in May 1945.

The cover page of Mike Botsko's combat diary

COMBAT DIARY
OF

MICHAEL BOTSKO
35091848

HOME ADDRESS:

1645 CAROLINA ST.

GARY, INDIANA

U.S.A.

MISSION #1

Date:	**Saturday, October 7, 1944**
Plane:	**#922 "The Gangs All Here"**
Target:	**Zwieckau, Germany**
Take Off:	**0740 Hours**

Well here I am all ready to start my tour of operations in the ETO and I'm really not ashamed to say that I'm scared of my first mission.

This first mission came as a surprise to me because I was the only enlisted man from our crew to fly today. Lt. Graves' ball-turret gunner was grounded so I'm to fly in his place.

The charge of quarters woke us up at some ungodly hour in the morning and said that breakfast was at 0300 hours. I was really sleepy but I finally managed to get up and get on the truck that would take us to the mess hall. For breakfast we had powdered eggs (which I hate), fried potatoes, cereal, bread and butter, and coffee.

After breakfast we were taken to operations for our briefing which was at 0430 hours. After that we got all of our flying equipment and went down to the plane. Our guns are in a tent near the plane so we wiped the oil off the guns and put them in the plane. I also had to check my turret, oxygen supply and ammunition. We still had a little time before take-off so after I met the rest of the crew I laid down in the tent and fell asleep.

At 0740 hours we took off and at last I was on my way. I didn't have to get in my turret until we assembled and were half way across the English Channel.

Everything was going along all right until we got into Germany. Number 3 engine started to act up and we couldn't keep up with the formation so the pilot ordered the bombardier to drop the bombs immediately so that we could keep up.

About twenty minutes before we hit the bomb run the group just behind us was hit by Jerry fighters. Those boys really caught hell because I counted eleven Forts go down in flames and two went down smoking. I didn't see any chutes get out of those planes. At the same time the group to our left went through a flak area and one Fort was hit. I followed that plane all the way down and saw six chutes get out of it.

When we came to the target we found the primary all smoked up by bombs dropped before us so we went to the secondary target which was an aircraft repair shop at Zwieckau, Germany. The rest of the planes in our group dropped their bombs and hit the target dead center.

On our way back the lead navigator had us twenty miles off course and when we were almost out of Germany we ran into a flak barrage over Munster and it knocked down one of our planes. Ted Golan of Chicago, a very good friend of mine, was flying extra waist gunner in that plane. No chutes were reported seen, so he must be done for. I went through gunnery school and R.T.U. with him. In that same flak area six more of our planes had some engines knocked out. We didn't run into any more trouble after that and I was really thankful when we landed.

We inspected the ship and found one flak hole in our vertical fin and the next day one of the ground crew gave me the flak as a souvenir of my first mission.

Landed: **1550 Hours**

Flying Time: **8 Hours 10 Minutes**

SATURDAY OCT 7, 1944

Reich Hit By 5,000 Aircraft

Germany underwent its greatest aerial assault of the war Saturday when more than 5,000 Allied bombers, mostly Fortresses and Liberators of the U.S. Strategic Air Forces, and fighters struck from Britain, France and Italy at key industrial and communications points from east to west and north to south.

The combined strength of more than 1,400 British-based bombers and upwards of 800 Italy-based B17s and B24s comprised the largest U.S. bomber force ever dispatched on a single operation.

Third Day in Row

This was the third successive day of large-scale operations by the Eighth Air Force and the biggest attacking force since June 20 when over 1,500 Eighth heavies went out.

The Eighth's losses were 51 bombers and 15 fighters against the destruction of 49 enemy craft in the air and on the ground, including four jet-propelled Nazi fighters.

Two Me262s were shot down by 1/Lt. Urban L. Drew, P51 pilot from Detroit, who became the first Eighth Fighter Command pilot to score a double kill over the Nazis' new type of interceptor in one day.

Maj. Richard E. Conner, P47 pilot from Vicksburg, Miss., also bagged an Me262, while three P51 pilots—1/Lts. Elmer A. Taylor, of Green Forest, Ark., Everett N. Farrell, of Superior, Ariz., and 2/Lt. Willard G. Erkamp, of Eagle Rock, Cal.—shared in destroying an Me163 jet-propelled fighter.

Oil Plants Hit

Escorted by more than 900 Thunderbolts, Mustangs and Lightnings of the Eighth and Ninth Air Forces, the Eighth heavies ranged over central, eastern and northeastern Germany, hammering synthetic oil plants at Politz, near the Baltic Sea: Ruhland, Magdeburg, Bohlen, Merseburg and Lutzkendorf. The latter three are in the Leipzig area, and Ruhland is northeast of Dresden.

Other targets included a Krupp tank works at Magdeburg; tank plants, aeroengine plant and locomotive works at Kassel; a chemical and explosive works at Clausthal-Zellerfeld, south of Brunswick; a Focke-Wulf 190 repair depot, airdrome and a motor transport plant at Zwickau, south of Leipzig, and an airfield at Nordhausen.

Striking simultaneously from the south, the 15th Air Force heavies, shepherded by nearly 400 fighters, pounded two oil refineries and an oil storage depot in the Vienna area.

Meantime, over 800 Lancasters and Halifaxes of the RAF Bomber Command, with fighter escort, smashed at the Nazi reinforcement centers of Emmerich and Kleve in western Germany, while other Lancasters carried out a low-level attack on the dykes guarding Walcheren Island.

Ninth Supports Armies

More than 300 Marauders and Havocs of the Ninth Air Force Saturday plastered bridges and supply points servicing enemy troops battling the U.S. First and Third Armies.

Ninth fighter-bombers in great strength ranged through the Rhine Valley and behind the German armies from Saarbrucken to Dusseldorf, bombing and strafing airfields, canals laden with supply barges, railroads and numerous artillery positions. About 200 enemy fighters were encountered.

Bad weather curtailed activity yesterday by British-based U.S. heavies.

MISSION #2

Date:	**Saturday, October 14, 1944**
Plane:	**#002 "Bums Aweigh"**
Target:	**Cologne, Germany**
Take Off:	**0822 Hours**

Once again I'm about to start on another mission and I'm still not ashamed to say that I'm as scared as hell. This time they woke us up at 0400 hours so we got one more hour of sleep than on the first mission. This will be my second mission and the first one for the rest of the enlisted men in our crew. After breakfast and briefing we were taken out to the plane where we cleaned our guns and got the rest of the plane ready to take off.

Well, we finally took off at 0822 hours and we assembled into formation at 16,000 feet over the field and then we were on our way. After we crossed the English Channel we flew over Dunkirk and for the first time I saw what that place really went through, and from what I saw it really went through a lot of hell.

We also went over Brussels, Belgium and from there we were on the bomb run. We were told that there would be quite a bit of flak over the target so everyone was pretty nervous. We were surprised though because there was very little flak over the target, but what there was of it was pretty darned accurate.

While over the target two planes from our group collided and I didn't see any chutes get out of them.

On our way back home we ran into two more flak barrages but it wasn't so bad because most of it was very inaccurate. When we got down and inspected the ship for flak holes we found seven of them and they were very small ones.

Landed:	**1523 Hours**
Flying Time:	**7 Hours 1 Minute**

MISSION #3

Date: **Tuesday, October 17, 1944**

Plane: **#120 "Punchy-Anna"**

Target: **Cologne, Germany**

Take Off: **0615 Hours**

Number 3 mission coming up and this is really supposed to be a honey.

They woke us up at 0200 hours and all of us were really dead tired and sleepy. Sometime I wish I hadn't even gone to bed. I didn't get but a few hours of sleep.

We were briefed on the same target as before so we thought it would be nothing but a milk-run.

We've been hitting this target so much because it has such an important rail center and it's in direct contact with Aachen, which is where our troops have been slowed down quite considerably by the Huns. A few more raids on Cologne and I think it should be wiped off the map.

This time we had a different route and we went over the Zuider Zee then turned south and hit Cologne. The flak over the target today was a little worse than the other day. One plane in our group was hit and no chutes were seen out of it.

When we landed I looked over the ship and there were quite a few flak holes in it.

Landed: **1330 Hours**

Flying Time: **7 Hours 15 Minutes**

MISSION #4

Date:	**Wednesday, October 25, 1944**
Plane:	**#120 "Punchy-Anna"**
Target:	**Hamburg, Germany**
Take Off:	**0928 Hours**

Today they woke us up at 0430 hours and we had breakfast at 0500. The briefing was at 0630 hours and it really wasn't much of a briefing at all today. They just told us that we would hit a repair shop for jet-propelled planes and that there would be a lot of fighters in the area so we were to be on the look-out for them.

After cleaning our guns and putting them in the plane we had some hot cocoa and cake and then we took off. Everyone sweated out the take-off because the weather was so bad that we had to take-off on instruments and climb until we got out of the fog.

Another thing we were sweating out was the pilot. Lt. Brooks was grounded today so we flew with a pilot that we didn't know anything about.

After assembling at 12,000 feet we were on our way for another mission.

We left England way up north somewhere and most of our flight was over the North Sea. We finally hit enemy territory and everyone was pretty nervous because of the briefing we had. S-2 also told us that there wouldn't be any flak over the target, but as the pilot said never expect to go over any target without flak because it can't be done.

We started over the target and I swear that I never saw so much flak in all my life. It seemed to me that we could let our wheels down and land on it, that's just how thick it was. We were down right lucky today though because we didn't lose any ships and ours just had one hole in the left wing.

We were in enemy territory for just one hour and then we were on our way back home. When we got over England we found it was fogged down even more than when we took off.

We were really scared because just 3 days ago two of our planes collided killing everyone in the ships. Three of the guys were very good friends of ours and slept in our barracks... "Arkey", "Ziggy" and Boling.

I bet that every one of our guys prayed just a little and that's what brought us down all right.

We finally landed and were thankful for that and we all hope that we don't have to go through that again.

Landed: **1628 Hours**

Flying Time: **7 Hours**

This is a blank page.

MISSION #5

Date: **Thursday, October 26, 1944**

Plane: **#120 "Punchy-Anna"**

Target: **Bielefeld, Germany**

Take Off: **1048 Hours**

Here I am ready to take you on another mission and this one really isn't bad.

They woke us up at 0600 hours today so none of us were very sleepy, just a little tired because of yesterday's mission.

We went over Amsterdam and the Zuider Zee and were escorted by P-51s all the way over there and back.

Our bomb load was four incendiaries and eight five-hundred pounders but I couldn't see the bomb hits because there were clouds below us and we dropped the bombs by PFF.

There was very little flak over the target and it was very inaccurate. I think that the chaff we're dropping is helping to mess up the enemy radar system a lot.

On our way back we saw a lot of B-24s going the opposite way so they must be hitting the same target as we hit.

We didn't have any more trouble on our way back so here's another mission finished.

Landed: **1725 Hours**

Flying Time: **6 Hours 37 Minutes**

MISSION #6

Date: **Monday, October 30, 1944**

Plane: **#002 "Bums Aweigh"**

Target: **Munster, Germany**

Take Off: **0945 Hours**

We got up at 0500 hours this morning and our crew was all pretty tired because most of us went out the night before and we got in pretty late.

Today just seemed to be our bad day and everything went wrong. First of all when we started off we didn't have any hydraulic pressure and we all started to worry about landing with no brakes – that would really be tough.

Well after we assembled and started off we got half way across the English Channel when our inter-phone system went out. Al the radio operator immediately started looking for the trouble and finally found it in the upper turret jack box, so the only way to fix it was to put that jack box on "command", so our inter-phones would work leaving Pennington without an inter-phone.

When we got near enemy territory I got into my ball turret and everything worked just fine for a few minutes, then my azimuth clutch froze on the out position and I couldn't get it back in to save my soul. Seeing that I couldn't get it fixed I notified the pilot and told him that I would crank it around by hand.

We had an escort of P-47s all the way over the target and back home again.

When we finally got over the target we found it was covered with clouds so we had to drop our bombs by PFF and I think that we did pretty good and what surprised us was that there was no flak over the target.

When we started on our way back we saw one plane in our group that couldn't get his bomb bay doors closed and another plane with engine problems.

Well this mission wasn't so bad but I hope I never have to crank my turret around again.

Landed: **1540 Hours**

Flying Time: **5 Hours 55 Minutes**

This is a blank page.

MISSION #7

Date: **Thursday, November 2, 1944**

Plane: **#354 "Flak Shy"**

Target: **Merseburg, Germany**

Take Off: **0837 Hours**

They really brought this mission up in a hurry because we just had two and a half hours between breakfast and take-off.

We all hurried around but we finally took off all right and we were really glad of that. We were all feeling good too because we were flying a new plane that just had ten missions on it.

Well to go on with my little story everything was going along just fine until we crossed the German border then our number two and three engines started smoking. The pilots flying the planes on both of our wings saw the engines smoking then started siding away from us because they thought that we were going to blow up or something.

Lt. Brooks feathered number three engine but number two couldn't be feathered so we dropped out of formation and started back home alone when we were just 30 minutes from the target. Oil shot out of both engines then number two caught fire and exploded, shooting parts all over the sky. Two pieces hit the pilot's window but he was lucky because the window was bullet-proof. One piece came through the side of the ship and hit the pilot in the elbow, but it didn't hurt him. Even though the engine exploded the prop still kept going around. Meanwhile the bombardier was looking around for a target to drop his bombs on. He finally dropped them and I saw them go down. He hit a canal, some railroads and a few houses.

We were all alone up there with no escort or anything and we were really scared that we would be jumped by Jerry fighters.

Al the radio operator was sending Q.D.M.s and S.O.S.s like mad and the rest of the crew was praying for an escort, but still no soap.

We were still over Germany and started to lose altitude so the pilot told us to prepare to bail-out, but when we got down to 10,000 feet we stopped losing altitude so we all got back on our guns.

Just before we hit the Zuider Zee, Smitty saw a Jerry twin-engine fighter take off from the ground and start up after us, but just then six P-47s came around and chased the Jerry away. The P-47s were sent to escort us in and we were really thankful for that.

Everything went along all right after that until we hit the English Channel. We started losing altitude again so the pilot ordered us to throw out everything, so we threw out our flak suits, flak helmets, guns, ammunition, camera and radio parts. I started to get rid of the ball turret and had everything except two bolts when the pilot said to save the ball because we weren't losing any more altitude and we were all thankful of that.

We finally hit the English coast and found everything closed in except a B-24 base on the coast so we started circling in and had Al radio the base for a weather report and instructions. The report finally came through and they told us to come in because the weather over the base was pretty clear, so flying in at 3,000 ft. we went on home.

We had a pretty big crowd waiting for us to land and Lt. Brooks made the most beautiful landing I've ever seen with just two engines running.

After we stopped we inspected the plane and found number two and three engines were burned out due to mechanical failure. It wasn't the ground crew's fault because the ship shouldn't have flown in the first place because the 200 hour inspection wasn't up to date.

After putting our equipment away we went to interrogation and made out our reports, then had a whiskey to straighten us out. Then we had some coffee and sandwiches and were taken back to our barracks by truck.

When we got back to the barracks Smitty's right hand started to hurt so the doc looked at it and found that he had a couple of chipped bones, so he will be grounded for a few days.

Landed: **1519 Hours**

Flying Time: **7 Hours 18 Minutes**

Luftwaffe Up, Loses 130 Planes

THURSDAY Nov. 2, 1944

For the first time in weeks the not-so-down-and-out Luftwaffe showed itself in great strength yesterday, and, according to preliminary reports Eighth Air Force fighters set a new record for a one-day bag by shooting down 130 enemy craft. Another 25 Nazi planes were destroyed on the ground.

The last time the Luftwaffe came up en masse was Sept. 11, when Eighth fighters clipped all their previous single-day records by shooting down 116 enemy planes.

As many as 400 Jerries were encountered yesterday by more than 900 Thunderbolts and Mustangs, which escorted over 1,100 Fortresses and Liberators in their attack on synthetic-oil plants in the Ruhr and at Merseburg in central Germany, as well as rail facilities at Bielefeld and Rheine, and other targets in western Germany.

Preddy's Men Get 24

The Mustang squadron led by Maj. George E. Preddy, of Greensboro, N.C., who is the top active Eighth fighter pilot in the ETO, shot down 24 Nazi craft to cop the day's squadron honors.

The 55th Fighter Group, a P51 outfit, led by Maj. Eugene E. Ryan, of Darien, Conn., tangled with over 75 single-engine Jerries which were "ganging up" on one bomber force over Merseburg, and claimed bagging 19 for the loss of one Mustang.

The heavies' gunners reported getting their share of additional "kills," shooting down 53.

Sgt. William E. Grose, of Hico, W. Va., ball-turret gunner on the Fort Little Chum, said: "I saw about eight FW190s sweep in toward the rear of our formation. I saw two of the Jerries go down."

2/Lt. Thomas Radonski, of Milwaukee, Wis., bombardier on the Fort That's All, Jack, reported: "As we were leaving the target area, three jet-propelled fighters broke out of a light haze in front of us. One, a light-green plane with black crosses, came in at us. At about 800 yards I opened fire. He was right in the middle of his turn, and seemed to be hanging in mid-air. That's where I got him."

FORT'S DIVE TO DEATH

FLYING Fortress screams down on fire after a direct shell hit during a raid on a German oil plant. The shell tore off the plane's nose and one engine, whose propeller can be seen flying into space.

This is a blank page.

MISSION #8

Date: **Saturday, November 4, 1944**

Plane: **#809 "Idiot's Delight"**

Target: **Rhur Valley, Germany**

Take Off: **0850 Hours**

Before I go on with this account I'd like to point out that this is not a bombing mission we're going on.

Twelve of our ships are going to be dropping chaff to mess up the German radar systems. In that way their anti-aircraft guns won't be very accurate against the rest of the planes that are dropping bombs.

Today we're acting as a screening force for a B-24 outfit of the 2nd division. We all like to go on the screening missions because we have plenty of fighter escort and we don't fly right over the target, so we hardly ever go through any flak areas.

Each ship carried 36 boxes of chaff and when we started to drop it the planes were all in one long line and it was really a beautiful sight to see.

We considered this a pretty easy mission because we didn't see any flak or enemy fighters. I hope we get more of these missions.

Smitty didn't fly today because of his injured hand.

Landed: **1417 Hours**

Flying Time: **5 Hours 27 Minutes**

MISSION #9

Date: **Thursday, November 9, 1944**

Plane: **#922 "One Man's Family"**

Target: **Saarbrucken, Germany**

Take Off: **0640 Hours**

Today we're going on a pretty important mission because we're supposed to be a big help to the ground forces.

They got us up pretty early this morning and since some of the revetments are being fixed our ships were parked on one of the runways so we had to take our guns from the tents out to the runways and that was a pretty long way to go. Smitty is still grounded so we've got another waist gunner flying with us.

We are carrying eight 1,000 lb. armor-piercing bombs to knock out some 155 mm enemy gun forts. Their forts are supposed to be pretty hard to knock out because the walls are said to be about 9 feet thick.

We got to our target and it was all clouded over so we didn't drop our bombs there. Instead we went to the secondary target which were some rail yards at Saarbrucken. We finally dropped our bombs there and went through a moderate flak area and we didn't lose any ships.

As soon as we left the target Lt. Heilborn asked for an oxygen check and everyone answered except the waist gunner, so he told Al to go see what was wrong. When Al got there he found the waist gunner on the floor so Al gave him some emergency oxygen and called the bombardier to tell him what was wrong. Lt. Heilborn immediately went back and with the help of Al they started to give the waist gunner artificial respiration.

After about 15 minutes the gunner still didn't show any signs of recuperation so Lt. Brooks started to take the ship down to a lower altitude. We all started taking turns giving the gunner artificial respiration and we worked for 2 ¾ hours on him. Al radioed the base telling them of our trouble so when we landed we had a couple of doctors ready to take over but it was useless because the waist gunner was already dead. The gunner's name was Samuel Clark and he was from Kansas, and we don't know what he died from.

Landed: **1330 Hours**

Flying Time: **6 Hours 50 Minutes**

Note

Samuel Clark's funeral was on Tuesday, November 14. His crew, our crew and a lot of his friends went to the funeral and it was really beautiful. There were quite a few other of our boys also being buried that same day so a lot of people were there.

Each casket was covered with an American flag, and when the chaplain read each name their friends attending the funeral saluted him, then a firing squad fired a salute for them and taps were played.

Clark was a nice guy, and even though we didn't know him very well we all miss him now.

This is a blank page.

MISSION #10

Date: **Tuesday, November 21, 1944**

Plane: **#162 "Old Glory"**

Target: **Merseburg, Germany**

Take Off: **0750 Hours**

Looks like another pretty rough mission ahead and most everyone is scared. We're supposed to bomb a synthetic oil plant and a jet plane factory, so we're all expecting to get a lot of flak and a hell of a lot of jet fighters.

We finally took off at 0750 hours and were on our way. Half way across the English Channel Chet and Smitty noticed their oxygen drop down pretty fast but then it stopped and didn't drop any more.

When we got into Germany we got a radio call telling us that the clouds dropped down to 19,000 feet over Merseburg. To go over the target at that altitude would be murder, so we turned around and headed for home and would drop our bombs on any target of opportunity.

After flying over Germany for what seemed to be ages to me we made three 360° turns and finally dropped our bombs. I watched them go down and they hit a factory, some railroad tracks and a bridge.

While on our way home everything was going along fine until we came to the coast, where we caught a little flak but it wasn't bad.

This is the second time that I've started for Merseburg and as of yet I haven't been anywhere near it.

Landed: **1520 Hours**

Flying Time: **7 Hours 30 Minutes**

MISSION #11

Date: **Wednesday, November 29, 1944**

Plane: **#037 "Liberty Run"**

Target: **Misburg, Germany**

Take Off: **0939 Hours**

We really thought we were going to get it today and I'm not kidding.

At our briefing S-2 told us to expect a lot of enemy fighters but luckily for us we didn't encounter any.

Today I saw more friendly fighters than I ever saw before, and each group of bombers had one group of fighters for close escort, and there were also some more groups of escorts around the target as well.

We dropped our bombs visually today and I saw them hit the target and start a lot of fires.

The flak over the target was moderate and fairly accurate.

Landed: **1650 Hours**

Flying Time: **7 Hours 20 Minutes**

MISSION #12

Date: **Thursday, November 30, 1944**

Plane: **#162 "Old Glory"**

Target: **Merseburg, Germany**

Take Off: **0900 Hours**

At briefing when they said our target was Merseburg I just about got sick because the boys who went over there lately have really been catching hell, from both flak and fighters. So when I put my guns in I was especially careful because if we got hit by Jerries I wanted both of my guns to be in perfect working order.

Our bomb load was eighteen 250 pound R.D.X.s and two smoke bombs.

Everything was going along alright until we came within sight of the target. That's when I got scared because the flak looked so heavy that it wasn't even funny. It was just like the Stars and Stripes said, you couldn't even see the planes on the other side of the target.

We came up on the bomb run and the bombardier opened the bomb bay doors. Then the flak got up to us and it was really thick and accurate. It was bouncing our plane all around and a piece of it hit the instruments of number one engine. The co-pilot saw the oil and fuel pressure drop down to zero so he feathered the engine without telling the pilot about it.

We got directly over the target and the bombardier dropped his bombs, but because a piece of flak cut some wires in the bomb bay only half of our bombs dropped. So with one engine feathered and half of our bombs still with us we couldn't keep up with the formation and we started to lose altitude. Flak was still knocking the plane all to hell. I saw our bombs hit the target, and one was a direct hit on a factory and I saw a big sheet of flame shoot a couple hundred of feet into the air.

One piece of flak came through the waist and it cut a lot of electrical wires. Another piece came through the tail and hit Chester's flak suit, scaring the hell out of him. I also saw one piece come through the bottom of the left wing that made a hole as big as this paper I'm writing on.

We were still carrying bombs and really lagged back a long way from the rest of the group. After we finally got out of the flak the bombardier got a piece of wire and started dropping bombs one at a time. Luckily we had a lot of fighter escort so we weren't jumped by any enemy fighters (thank goodness).

By the time we got out of enemy territory all but four of our bombs were gone, so when we got over the English Channel we dropped the rest of them. We finally got home alright and I counted twenty-two flak holes in our ship.

A guy named Fisher who was flying ball-turret in the ship on our left had a piece of flak shatter the glass, spraying pieces all over his face and in his eyes.

Another plane from our field received a direct hit and it blew up in midair.

Landed: **1725 Hours**

Flying Time: **8 Hours 25 Minutes**

This is a blank page.

MISSION #13

Date: **Monday, December 4, 1944**

Plane: **#995 "Cisco's Kids"**

Target: **Kassel, Germany**

Take Off: **0830 Hours**

Today's mission was pretty good and we hit the rail yards at Kassel.

We looked around for Jerry fighters because the last time we hit Kassel they jumped a few of the groups.

Once again the lead navigator screwed up and took us off course and we ended up over Frankfurt, and boy the flak really came up there and we luckily just hit the edge of it. We got one hole in our right wing that was about as big as a half-dollar.

When we were headed to the target we had one hell of a tail wind that was reported to be about a hundred miles and hour. We were going so fast that we were overshooting most of our turns. Then coming back home it really took us a long time because we had to buck the strong head wind and it sometimes looked as if we were standing still.

We finally got home though so that's another mission I've completed.

Landed: **1700 Hours**

Flying Time: **8 Hours 30 Minutes**

Two of the crew members

This is a blank page.

MISSION #14

Date: **Monday, January 1, 1945**

Plane: **#098 "Hell's Baby"**

Target: **Göttengen, Germany**

Take Off: **0730 Hours**

Here it is the first of the new year and they really gave us a rough one to start off.

When we started to assemble over the field this morning it was still dark, and to see all those planes flying around really scared me all to hell. While assembling, two planes collided and went down in flames, and no one got out. We finally got assembled and headed off for the North Sea. We were just at about 5,000 feet over the water when we saw another plane explode and one going down to ditch. The radio operator sent in a position report to air-sea rescue and I hope to hell that those boys get picked up.

Before I go on any further I'd like to say that today is the first mission I'm going on where I'm flying as a waist gunner. Lt. Punzo, our former co-pilot, is flying his first mission as 1st pilot.

Now to go on with my story...

We flew over the North Sea until we got well above Germany. We then sighted a couple of ports that were laying down heavy smoke screens, obviously they were hiding something important. We finally turned south and were going down to our target when we sighted flak. It was pretty heavy in one particular spot so I knew that was indeed our target. We went through all that heavy flak and didn't drop our bombs. The pilot called us and said that we were going to the secondary target.

Our bomb bay doors got stuck and we couldn't get them up, so the engineer had to crank them up by hand.

When we got to the target our bomb bay doors were working again. We were directly over the target and everyone was quiet over the inter-phone when the bombardier yelled out "bombs away!". I thought he was crazy because we didn't have any flak around us at all.

Then we turned west again and we were on our way home. It was really a beautiful day for bombing because there were hardly any clouds in the sky, and you could look down and see everything. There was a lot of snow on the ground, and when we flew over the front lines most of the small towns looked as if they were just recently bombed. I asked the pilot what happened down there, and he said that for the last few days fighters were strafing and dropping wing bombs.

The bombardier said there was flak coming up in front of us, so we skirted around to the left and ran into some that wasn't real heavy but damned accurate.

We got near our field and the weather started to close in, so we went in one element at a time (three ships). We finally landed and here we are.

When we went to interrogation we were told that our screening force was hit by enemy fighters and one of our groups lost six ships. One of them was from our own squadron.

S/Sgt. Fitzpatrick, one of the guys in our barracks, went to the hospital with plexiglas in his eyes.

Landed: 1630 Hours

Flying Time: 9 Hours

This is a blank page.

MISSION #15

Date: **Friday, January 5, 1945**

Plane: **#809 "Idiot's Delight"**

Target: **Dumplefeld, Germany**

Take Off: **0820 Hours**

Here I am on another mission and I just hope to God that it isn't very rough.

Today our crew flew together for a change, but we had a ball-turret operator who was being baptized to combat flying. His name is S/Sgt. Roman and he is a Slovak from Wilkes-Barre, Pennsylvania.

The mission we're going on could really be easy, but these damned arm-chair generals always seem to make it rough for us. They fly us all over Germany to hit a target that isn't very far away.

We got off to a good start, but then when we entered Germany our number one engine started to run away and Lt. Punzo really had a job to keep it in control.

Our target was a German training camp for troops going into the front lines, so we were carrying twelve 500 pound bombs.

We got over the target and the flak was very meager. I saw just one burst from the waist position, and the other gunners saw about 10 or 12 bursts all together.

This was a pretty easy mission and now it's just one less to go for me.

Landed: **1640 Hours**

Flying Time: **8 Hours 10 Minutes**

MISSION #16

Date: **Saturday, January 6, 1945**

Plane: **#809 "Idiot's Delight"**

Target: **Cologne, Germany**

Take Off: **0730 Hours**

They woke us up pretty early this morning and I was really tired because I didn't go to bed very early last night. Oh well, a mission is a mission and I can't do anything about it.

We took off in the dark and I really hate that. We flew up to 14,000 feet and started to assemble there. Lt. Punzo told us to take it easy on our oxygen because we may need to come back home all the way on oxygen.

We finally started off and it was really cold, so we were really throwing off a hell of a lot of contrails, which isn't good because the Jerry fighters like to sneak up on us in them. I'll have to admit though that they really look pretty.

Our escort met us at the designated location and they really looked nice to us because the Jerrys have been coming up lately.

The primary target was a bridge just outside the city but it was clouded up, so we headed to the secondary target, which were the rail yards inside the city.

Our tail and upper turret gunners saw some planes having a dog fight behind us. We got our bomb bay doors open and the lead ship screwed up, so we went over the target without dropping our bombs. We were all madder than hell because there was plenty of flak up there, but we couldn't do anything else but make a 360° turn and go over the target again.

We went over the target for the second time and it looked as though we were the only plane around, and it seemed as though even our escort went away.

When we went over the target this time our low squadron straggled behind us a little and we didn't encounter any flak, but the low squadron really caught hell. When Smitty the toggalier dropped the bombs our ship really gave a big lurch because he salvoed all the bombs (two 1,000 pounders and two 2,000 pounders).

When we got back to our base we had to circle the field for an hour because a plane that was landing before us blew out a tire and it took that long to tow the plane off the runway. So that's another mission done and just nineteen more to go.

On our way to the target we saw quite a few V-2 rockets taking off.

Landed: **1540 Hours**

Flying Time: **8 Hours 10 Minutes**

This is a blank page.

MISSION #17

Date: **Sunday, January 7, 1945**

Plane: **#809 "Idiot's Delight"**

Target: **Coblenz, Germany**

Take Off: **0836 Hours**

Everything seemed all messed up this morning but it all turned out alright in the end.

I was scheduled to fly with another crew today but Lt. Punzo didn't like that so he got me changed to his crew. Then at briefing he got sick so they got us another pilot and that left Smitty and me with a mixed-up crew.

At the briefing we were all warned to watch out for "intruders". Intruders are Jerries who try to sneak into England with our planes and follow us to our field and then try to shoot us up when we're going in for a landing.

We took off all right and were flying in the number two position, both high element and the high squadron. Our bomb load was twelve 500 pounders and our gas load was 2,780 gallons.

We assembled over the field at 17,000 feet and then we started on our way to the target. Everything was going along just fine, but we were all scared as hell because Coblenz is supposed to be a big flak trap.

Just before we crossed the front lines a plane from another field tagged along with us and flew on our right wing. Our navigator was pretty excited because this was his very first mission and he was really a lot of fun.

We finally got on the bomb run and the bomb bay doors were opened up and Al the radio operator started to drop chaff. Everyone was quiet over the inter-phone, and then someone yelled out "Flak at 1 o'clock low!". I started looking around for it but couldn't see it, and then the ship gave a little lurch and the bombardier yelled out "bombs away!". After that we were all a little relieved because we were flying on our own time then. The bomb bay doors closed and we were on our way home.

We kept our altitude until we got over England and then we let down through the clouds and it was really a mess because of ground haze. If you looked toward the sun you couldn't see a thing, but when looking away from it visibility was good and we landed safely.

Landed: **1602 Hours**

Flying Time: **7 Hours 27 Minutes**

This is a blank page.

MISSION #18

Date: **Saturday, January 13, 1945**

Plane: **#564 "Merry Widow"**

Target: **Karlsruhe, Germany**

Take Off: **0905 Hours**

Today was supposed to be a pretty good mission for us and it proved to be so.

We were out for a bridge that carried quite a bit of traffic right up to the front lines.

On our way to the target we saw a few rockets shot up from Holland. We got over the target and the flak was moderate and below us. We were flying in the high squadron and the low squadron got all the flak. Today was the first time I saw red flak and it looked really pretty to me.

We hit the target dead center and I'm really glad of that because now we don't have to go to that place again.

When we started back our radio operator got a message from division for us to be diverted to another field because of bad weather at our base. Most of us landed at an R.A.F. field called Weston Zoyland. We didn't have it too bad there but we thought it could have been better.

Landed: **1650 Hours**

Flying Time: **7 Hours 45 Minutes**

We took off from Weston Zoyland the next day at 1130 hours and we flew home alone.

Landed: **1225 Hours**

Flying Time: **55 Minutes**

Total Flying Time: **8 Hours 40 Minutes**

Mid-air photos taken by Mike Botsko

MISSION #19

Date: **Monday, January 15, 1945**

Plane: **#564 "Merry Widow"**

Target: **Freiburg, Germany**

Take Off: **0825 Hours**

Today was a pretty easy mission but I still say that no mission is a "milk run" as some wise guys claim.

Our primary target was supposed to be a railroad bridge, but since it was covered by clouds we went to our secondary target which was a rail yard at Freiburg, which is right near the Swiss border. In fact it was so close that we could see Switzerland from where we were flying.

We got over the target and were very surprised because we didn't even see one burst of flak.

Capt. Brooks was flying off our right wing and they didn't drop their bombs so they made a second run on the target all alone.

Our fighter escort was really good and we didn't get any fighter opposition.

We got back alright and now I just have 16 more missions to go.

Landed: **1525 Hours**

Flying Time: **7 Hours**

MISSION #20

Date: **Wednesday, January 17, 1945**

Plane: **#564 "Merry Widow"**

Target: **Paderborn, Germany**

Take Off: **0935 Hours**

Today most of us guys were pretty mad because this is the third day in a row that we're flying as a "spare". Sometimes a spare will fly and sometimes they don't, but you still have to get up with the regular mission.

So there we are flying with our group and the number three plane of the low squadron of the high group falls out and we pull up to fill in its place.

S/Sgt. Andy Anderson was flying his last mission with us in the ball turret so he was pretty nervous, but we told him to calm down because our mission was supposed to be fairly easy. We were expecting just a little flak but we weren't sure about fighters.

There was quite a bit of clouds below us and there was a thick haze above us so if we got hit we would hardly know it.

When we got over the target I didn't see any flak, but some of the other guys reported about 12 or 13 bursts. I never saw so many Forts going over a target in all my life. I don't know where they all came from but they were there.

We got back to the home base alright and upon inspection of our plane we didn't find any holes from flak in it.

Landed: **1700 Hours**

Flying Time: **7 Hours 25 Minutes**

MISSION #21

Date: **Saturday, January 20, 1945**

Plane: **#564 "Merry Widow"**

Target: **Rheine, Germany**

Take Off: **0717 Hours**

Most everyone was pretty jittery today because at briefing we were told to look out for a lot of Jerry fighters.

Everything went along fine and we saw a little flak just before we came up on the target. We went to the secondary target and dropped our bombs with no trouble at all.

Just after we left the target I noticed 3 fighters at 3 o'clock level who started a pursuit curve. We all held our fire because they were too far away and we couldn't positively identify them. Then when they got to about 5 o'clock I recognized them and called out over the inter-phone, but it was too late. Chet was already firing at them, and they were some of our own P-51s. Chet was in the clear though because no friendly plane has the right to make a pursuit curve with it's nose pointing toward us for such a long time.

We bombed at 29,000 feet and that's the highest I've ever been in a B-17. The outside temperature was 56° below zero.

We got home alright and there was another ball turret operator who had finished up with us.

Landed: **1330 Hours**

Flying Time: **6 Hours 13 Minutes**

MISSION #22

Date: **Sunday, January 21, 1945**

Plane: **#564 "Merry Widow"**

Target: **Aschaffenburg, Germany**

Take Off: **0720 Hours**

This was another one of those missions that was made up in a hurry and I really hate that because you have to run around so much.

It had snowed like hell all of last night so everyone that wasn't flying was out cleaning the snow off of the runways. When Lt. Punzo was taxiing out to the runway his left wheel went off the perimeter track and we had to get a tractor to pull us out of the snow and mud. That little delay caused us to be the last ones to take off.

After we were formed everything was going along just fine and we saw a lot of flak coming up from Frankfurt which was over to our left. Our fighter escort was just perfect, and there were P-51s all over the sky, which is what we all like to see. We also saw one of the new English jet-propelled planes – them babies sure are fast!

After we got past the target the navigator passed out because his oxygen mask froze up, but the toggelier took very good care of reviving him.

This was a pretty easy mission but it was sure damn long.

Another mission over for me and all I have to go is 13 more.

Landed: **1630 Hours**

Flying Time: **9 Hours 10 Minutes**

MISSION #23

Date: **Sunday, January 28, 1945**

Plane: **#813 "Danny Boy"**

Target: **Cologne, Germany**

Take Off: **0805 Hours**

Once again we're going out and I sure hope to hell I can get my missions in and go home. I'm tired of this damned place.

We took off alright and everything was going along fine until just before we got to the target when we got a radio call that there were bandits (Jerry fighters) in the area. We weren't worried too much because our fighter escort was just perfect. There were P-51s all around us and to me they looked a lot better than anything I've ever seen.

I'm really starting to sweat these missions out because I'm so near being finished.

We got over the target and we got some flak and it wasn't much but it was damned accurate. To me it looked as though there were just about 8 or 9 flak guns down there.

On our way back "One Eye Willie" was out and sent up a few bursts that were really close.

Landed: **1555 Hours**

Flying Time: **7 Hours 50 Minutes**

MISSION #24

Date: **Monday, January 29, 1945**

Plane: **#564 "Merry Widow"**

Target: **Coblenz, Germany**

Take Off: **0805 Hours**

Just think, when I get back from this mission I'll just have 11 to go.

Everything went along alright until we got to the target where we got hit by quite a bit of flak and it was damned accurate. We didn't lose any ships but one bombardier was hit and hurt pretty bad. We did our bombing visually today so the chaff didn't do much good in messing up the radar systems.

We landed alright thank goodness and now I hope I can get my next missions in – I want to go home.

I won't be flying for awhile now because we're all going on leave except Lt. Heilborn as he doesn't have the required number of missions.

Gee but we all miss Roberts and would like to know if he's a P.W. or not.

Landed: **1606 Hours**

Flying Time: **8 Hours 1 Minute**

MISSION #25

Date: **Wednesday, February 14, 1945**

Plane: **#564 "Merry Widow"**

Target: **Dresden, Germany**

Take Off: **0825 Hours**

This is a pretty important mission because we're bombing a city and we're in direct support of the Russians. Our target is a big railroad yard that has a hell of a lot of traffic going to the Russian front.

We took off alright and ran into a little flak on our way to the target, but when we got to the target we didn't see any more.

The target was covered by scattered clouds so we dropped our bombs by instrument and then we made a sharp turn and as we were turning I looked out the waist window and I could see the bombs hitting. It really looked pretty seeing all those bombs hitting and all the incendiaries starting fires down there.

On our way back we ran into a little more flak but no damage was inflicted on us.

This was a pretty good mission but it was too damned long and I say that we should have landed on Russian soil, loaded up the next day, and then made another mission on our way back home.

Landed: **1725 Hours**

Flying Time: **9 Hours**

MISSION #26

Date: **Thursday, February 15, 1945**

Plane: **#639 "Topper"**

Target: **Dresden, Germany**

Take Off: **0720 Hours**

We're off on another one of these damn long missions and I really dread to start on it. Oh well, there isn't anything I can do about it but fly it.

We took off alright but after we got up we saw an explosion on our field and no other planes took off, so we got a radio message to proceed with our mission with just 14 other planes.

Everything went along just fine and when we got over the target we didn't see any flak or fighters so there we were on our way home. We got just a little flak near Frankfurt but it was very inaccurate and there wasn't enough to amount to very much.

When we landed we found out that one plane got caught in some prop wash on take-off and crashed into some barracks, killing 1 and injuring 16 in the barracks. When the bombs went off it killed 5 of the crew members. Another plane tried to take-off with locked controls and when it crashed it killed 6 other crew members.

I'm really sweating out my missions now and I just have 9 more to go.

Landed: **1623 Hours**

Flying Time: **9 Hours 3 Minutes**

MISSION #27

Date: **Wednesday, February 21, 1945**

Plane: **#564 "Merry Widow"**

Target: **Nuremburg, Germany**

Take Off: **0710 Hours**

We really got scared at briefing today because 2 missions were put up on the board. The first one was to Berlin, and the second one was to Nuremburg. They finally told us that we were going to Nuremburg and thank goodness for that.

On our way everything was going along alright until just before we reached the target and 4 flak guns started to fire at us and they were sure accurate. Our ship was the only one that got any battle damage.

We got to the target and dropped our bombs and didn't see any flak there so I was pretty happy. Then we got a radio message that there were bandits (Jerries) in the area so my morale dropped to about zero again. It wasn't bad though because we had a very good fighter escort.

We left enemy territory and were on our way home. We finally landed and now I have only 8 more to go.

Landed: **1610 Hours**

Flying Time: **9 Hours**

MISSION #28

Date: **Thursday, February 22, 1945**

Plane: **#144 "Jane"**

Target: **Wittemberge, Germany**

Take Off: **0815 Hours**

This was really a queer mission for us today because we were going to assemble over the field at 8,000 feet and then enter the enemy coast at 20,000 feet and after that drop down to 12,000 feet and go over the target at that altitude.

It was really an all out effort for the 8th Air Force because all the planes were going there and bombing rail yards in different little cities and our group got Wittemberge.

We were going along alright and we came to the target and dropped our bombs and really wiped that target out. We didn't get any flak but the group that was on our right side got hit by fighters and they lost a few planes, and over on our left side a P-51 blew up because of engine trouble.

On our way back we watched the P-51s do a lot of strafing. I saw two train engines get blown up and one oil or gas tank also.

Back at the base we kind of sweated the weather out because it was foggy but we landed alright.

Landed: **1635 Hours**

Flying Time: **8 Hours 20 Minutes**

MISSION #29

Date: **Friday, February 23, 1945**

Plane: **#564 "Merry Widow"**

Target: **Wurzburg, Germany**

Take Off: **0740 Hours**

Once again we are going on one of these low-level bombing runs and I don't like them one bit because if there's just one flak gun down there it's going to just knock the hell out of the whole outfit.

We took off today and it was really foggy. We climbed up to 10,000 feet and were still in fog, but we finally got through it and assembled and were off for the target. When the ball-turret gunner got into the turret he wasn't in it for more than 5 minutes when the wiring started to burn. So I pulled the emergency switch and put out the fire, then the gunner got out and had to stow his turret for the rest of the mission.

We got over the primary target and it was clouded over, so we got radio orders to keep going and to hit a target that was visual. We just kept going until we got away from the clouded areas. I had a camera in the waist gun position so I took pictures of flak and some other targets. Just before we arrived over our target I saw some P-51s strafing an air-field so I took some pictures of Jerry planes burning on the ground. I followed our bombs down to the ground and saw them hit the target and literally wipe it off the map.

On our way back our number four engine started to throw oil so we dropped out of formation and we were on our own. We started to drop down through the clouds and then ran into fog. We were flying about 100 feet off the ground and all of us were sweating it out. Thank goodness our pilot Lt. Punzo could really handle the plane, and that our navigator was really good in that he split the field right in two and we made a really good landing.

Now it's just one mission less to go.

Landed: **1655 Hours**

Flying Time: **9 Hours 15 Minutes**

This is a blank page.

MISSION #30

Date: **Saturday, February 24, 1945**

Plane: **#109 "Kokomo Kid"**

Target: **Hamburg, Germany**

Take Off: **0810 Hours**

We really got scared this morning at briefing because the briefing officer told us that the flak would really be intense over the target, so we were looking for most anything to happen.

Our take-off was scheduled for 6:30 but at the last instant they set it back for 2 more hours. The ship we were supposed to fly was messed up so we had to change ships. I really didn't like going on this mission because they had me down for tail-gunner and I've never flown that position before.

Everything went along just fine until we got a little flak thrown up at us when we passed near Bremen. Then when we got to the target a hell of a lot of flak was thrown up at us, and it was at our altitude but just a little off to our right.

We left the target and as we were on our way home I swear I never saw so many bombers going back home in all my life. B-24s and B-17s were all out in force so we must have done a hell of a lot of damage.

Landed: **1610 Hours**

Flying Time: **8 Hours**

MISSION #31

Date: **Sunday, February 25, 1945**

Plane: **#144 "Jane"**

Target: **Munich, Germany**

Take Off: **0645 Hours**

I really dreaded to start on this mission because I knew it was going to be long as hell and this was my 5th day of flying in a row.

On our way to the target we got a little flak at the front lines and we saw other planes dropping bombs and getting flak thrown up at them. When we were nearing our target we saw a lot of flak where other planes were headed to our same target. When we came up over the target the flak was coming up fast and it was really accurate. It bounced our ship all around but we didn't lose anyone. Lt. Heilborn was flying as lead bombardier and he really plastered the target.

We got on the other side of our target and one of our planes headed for Switzerland because of engine trouble. He went a little way but then had to turn around because he couldn't gain enough altitude to make it over the Alps. The men from that plane bailed out over friendly territory and I sure hope to God that they are all safe.

We landed safely and now I just have 4 more missions to go.

Both Lt. Punzo an S/Sgt. C. Bemis finished up today.

Landed: **1610 Hours**

Flying Time: **8 Hours**

MISSION #32

Date: **Thursday, March 1, 1945**

Plane: **#639 "Topper"**

Target: **Reutlingen, Germany**

Take Off: **1030 Hours**

Today looked like another pretty easy mission, and thank goodness they gave us a little more time to sleep because I really needed it.

We started for the runway when our tail-wheel blew out, so we pulled on the side and had the ground crew fix it for us. That little delay caused us to be the last ones to take off and we had to meet the rest of the group out at the coast. Once we met the group though everything was alright and we were flying deputy lead of the high squadron.

As soon as we hit the front lines we had about 20 bursts of flak thrown up at us but it wasn't very accurate. We hit our target visually and there wasn't any flak over it so we were all pretty darned happy about that.

On our way back we had a little more flak thrown up at us near the front lines and then we landed at our own base so now it's just 3 more to go.

Landed: **1830 Hours**

Flying Time: **8 Hours**

MISSION #33

Date: **Saturday, March 3, 1945**

Plane: **#638 "Cover Girl"**

Target: **Ruhland, Germany**

Take Off: **0535 Hours**

This is one mission that I'll never forget as long as I live, so I'll just start at the beginning.

We took off all right and everything went along just fine until we came to the target. We had a hell of a lot of flak over there and I was in the waist taking pictures of it with a movie camera. I don't know what happened but the lead bombardier didn't drop his bombs so we had to go through all of that damned flak over again.

This time we dropped our bombs and then we started making more circles over Germany while we were waiting for three other planes to drop their bombs. We finally headed for home and then started to sweat out our gas supply. We left the formation and were on our own.

The pilot told us to get ready to bail out. I put my G.I. boots on and then my flying boots, then I started to tighten my parachute harness.

We finally got over the lines and were over Belgium at 4,000 feet, so the pilot rang the bail-out bell, the toggelier kicked out the waist door and jumped, then the tail-gunner went out, then the ball-turret gunner, and I went out next. I tried to straighten out a little to stop tumbling and I looked up to see if I was clear of the plane, then I pulled my rip cord and the chute didn't open. I got scared as hell and started to tear my chute open. I grabbed the pilot-chute and threw it out, and then the rest of the chute popped open. It snapped me a little but I didn't mind it so much. I was pretty near the ground and then landed kind of hard. The wind dragged me along the ground a little, and I grabbed the lower shroud lines and spilled my chute. I then got out of my harness and an F.F.I. man with a rifle stopped me and I put up my hands. I said I was an American, and then he said to me "Oh, Merican, goot, goot".

I saw the engineer hit the ground about 400 yards from me, and the wind was dragging him so I ran over and spilled his chute. He couldn't get up because his right ankle was broken. The tail-gunner and the ball-turret gunner came over to us and by that time I had sent for an ambulance and the people there brought us some cognac and coffee.

About an hour later a jeep came by with a Lieutenant Colonel and a Corporal and they took me and the tail-gunner to get an ambulance. We went to a town named Dinant and got the ambulance and then stayed in the town and had something to eat. The radio operator and the toggelier showed up and we were questioned by the M.P.s and given a place to stay. We had 3 English pounds between us and traded it for 500 francs and went out to get something to drink.

The next afternoon we were taken to Brussels where we sure had a darned nice time.

On the 5th of March we were flown in a C-47 back to England.

Now you see what I mean by an experience that I'll never forget and I hope it never happens to me again.

Bailed Out: **1415 Hours**

Flying Time: **8 Hours 40 Minutes**

Note

The pilot landed the plane all alone with no engines running, and the rest of the crew bailed out.

A letter issued by the Duty Equipment Officer confirming Mike Botsko's parachute jump

(E-K-17)

Headquarters AAF Station No. 105
Office of the Personal Equipment Officer
APO 557

1 April 1945.

SUBJECT: Confirmation of Parachute Jump.

TO   : Chairman Caterpillar Club.

1. S/Sgt. Michael Botsko, 422nd Bombardment Squadron (H), 305th Bombardment Group (H), jumped from his aircraft to save his life on the third of March, 1945. S/Sgt. Botsko used an A-3 parachute, 24 foot canopy manufactured by the Reliance Manufacturing Company, serial number 42-817089

ALBERT C. BACA JR.
Captain, Air Corps,
Group Personal Equipment Officer.

MISSION #34

Date: **Sunday, March 11, 1945**

Plane: **#144 "Jane"**

Target: **Bremen, Germany**

Take Off: **0930 Hours**

Once again I'm off on another mission and I'm really getting near the end of my tour.

I kind of liked this mission because we had a little more time to sleep in the morning and it was a late take-off.

Everything went off just swell and today I'm flying in the ball-turret again because all the waist guns were taken out. We got off all right and I was even happy to fly in the ball – it could be that all the flak is affecting me or something.

Just before we hit enemy territory I got in the ball and both it and my guns were in perfect working order so I was happy.

We got over the target, dropped our bombs, and then the flak started to come up. There was sure a hell of a lot of it but it wasn't accurate and we just got two holes in our ship.

On our way back over England we almost had an accident when a British plane came right for us. It's lucky that our pilot dove the plane down to avoid getting hit.

I'm down now and I'm going to get grounded so that Jack and Bill can catch up to me as we want to go home together.

Landed: **1640 Hours**

Flying Time: **7 Hours 10 Minutes**

MISSION #35

Date: **Tuesday, March 20, 1945**

Plane: **#809 "Idiot's Delight"**

Target: **Hamburg, Germany**

Take Off: **1330 Hours**

This mission came up in a hurry and we had a very late take-off. Four of us in the ship were finishing up today and we were all pretty nervous about it.

Most of the way to the target was over water and we passed over one little island that had a Jerry airfield on it, so everyone was on the ball and really looking out for fighters.

We finally came over the target and were hit with a hell of a lot of flak. Then just after we dropped our bombs and turned off the target we got a call that there were bandits in the area. I saw the group behind us get hit by fighters and two Forts went down. Then we got hit by a couple of jet jobs, and I swear I never saw a plane as fast as those jets. I couldn't even keep my sights on them as they were so fast. Then our fighter escort came to our rescue and chased the jets away.

We didn't get into any more trouble on the way home and we were thankful for that.

Now we've finished our tour of operations in the E.T.O., so I think I'll just go get drunk tonight.

Landed: **2130 Hours**

Flying Time: **8 Hours**

Note

On March 24th I got a fighter confirmed. I got him on my last mission. He came in on our tail, then broke downward. I was firing all the while, and his engine caught fire and I saw him hit the silk.

A page from Mike Botsko's combat diary

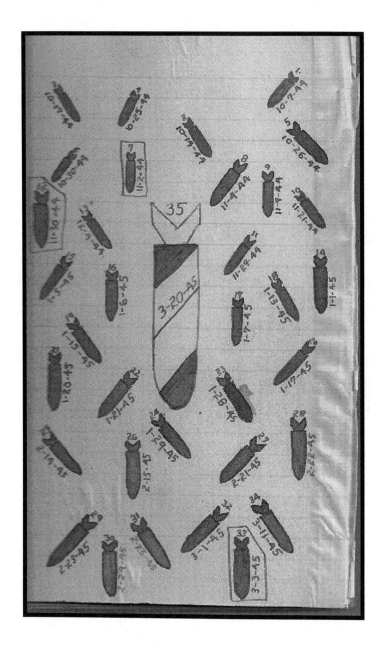

Epilogue

by R.J. Kluba

On April 25, 1945 the 305th Bombardment Group flew its final combat mission of the war. During their tour of duty the group flew a total of 337 missions, 9,231 sorties and carried a total bomb tonnage of 22,363 tons. A total of 154 aircraft were reported missing in action (MIA).

The war in Europe officially came to an end in May 1945, with the unconditional surrender of all German forces to the Allies in Berlin.

After Mike Botsko's discharge from the Army, he returned to his hometown of Gary, Indiana and found employment there as a tool & die maker. He was married in 1950 and had 2 children.

Tragically, Mike was killed in an auto accident in 1976 at the age of 53, and this transcriber deeply regrets that he never got to meet the man that wrote this incredible account of his war experiences. I married his daughter in 1987, which is how I learned about his service in World War II and his combat diary.

After initially leafing through the pages of the diary, and then reading and re-reading each captivating account of all 35 missions Mike flew, I realized that his story was such a significant and important part of our nation's history that it needed to be shared.

I am humbly grateful and say thank you to Mike, and to all those brave patriots like him, who have served our country and suffered, endured and sacrificed for the freedom of all Americans and the entire world.

Glossary of Terms

chaff	A radar countermeasure in which aircraft or other targets spread a cloud of small, thin pieces of aluminum, metallized glass fiber or plastic, which either appears as a cluster of secondary targets on radar screens or swamps the screen with multiple returns.
ETO	European Theatre of Operations
F.F.I.	French Forces of the Interior (aka. the French Resistance)
flak	Exploding shells fired from anti-aircraft guns positioned on the ground.
Fort	A nickname given to the B-17 "Flying Fortress" airplane.
Huns	Slang used as a disparaging term for German soldiers in World War II.
Jerry	A nickname given to Germans during World War II by soldiers and civilians of the Allied Forces nations.
PFF	Path Finder Force - a specially equipped radar navigation system devised by the British and improved by the Americans for targeting through heavy cloud cover.
P.W.	Prisoner of War
Q.D.M.	An aviation call sign used to request a magnetic heading to a station.
R.A.F.	Royal Air Force
R.D.X.	Research Department Explosive. One of the first manufactured 'plastic' explosives. It was widely used during World War II.
R.T.U.	Replacement Training Unit
S-2	Army staff in charge of intelligence - collects data on enemy movements, strengths, and battlefield deployments, and makes recommendations for command.
sortie	One mission or attack by a single plane.
S.O.S.	A code message or signal that means Save Our Ship.

Mike Botsko - October 1945

Mike Botsko   R.J. Kluba

November 5, 1944   November 5, 2011

"Freedom is the precious gift given by those alone who have the courage to defend it."

~ Pericles ~